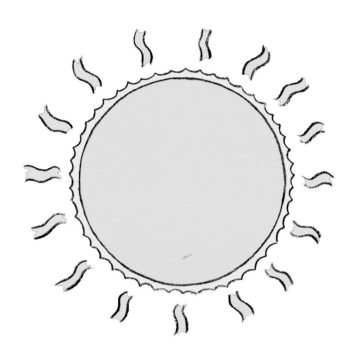

LEVEL 2 SCIENCE

LET'S READ AND FIND OUT

SUNSHINE
MAKES THE SEASONS

BY FRANKLYN M. BRANLEY · ILLUSTRATED BY MICHAEL REX

HARPER

An Imprint of HarperCollinsPublishers

To Teresa, my sunshine
—M.R.

The Let's-Read-and-Find-Out Science book series was originated by Dr. Franklyn M. Branley, Astronomer Emeritus and former Chairman of the American Museum of Natural History–Hayden Planetarium, and was formerly co-edited by him and Dr. Roma Gans, Professor Emeritus of Childhood Education, Teachers College, Columbia University. Text and illustrations for each of the books in the series are checked for accuracy by an expert in the relevant field. For more information about Let's-Read-and-Find-Out Science books, write to HarperCollins Children's Books, 195 Broadway, New York, NY 10007, or visit our website at www.letsreadandfindout.com.

Library of Congress Cataloging-in-Publication Data
Branley, Franklyn Mansfield, date.
  Sunshine makes the seasons / by Franklyn M. Branley ; illustrated by Michael Rex.—Newly illus-
trated ed.
    p.   cm.—(Let's-read-and-find-out-science. Stage 2)
  ISBN 978-0-06-238209-2
  1. Seasons—Juvenile literature. 2. Sunshine—Juvenile literature. [1. Seasons. 2. Sunshine.] I. Rex, Michael, ill. II.
Title. III. Series.
QB637.4.B73 2005   2003025457
508.2—dc22   CIP
                                                                                                                    AC

15 16 17 18 19 SCP 10 9 8 7 6 5 4 3 2 1
❖
Revised edition, 2016

SUNSHINE MAKES
THE SEASONS

Sunshine warms the earth.

If the sun stopped shining, the earth would get colder and colder. We would freeze. The whole earth would freeze.

The sun shines all through the year. But we are warmer in summer than in winter. The amount of sunshine makes the difference.

The earth spins around, or rotates, once in twenty-four hours. That's why we have day and night. When we are on the sun side of the earth, there is daylight. As the earth rotates, we turn away from the sun. There is sunset and then night.

At the same time that the earth spins, it goes around the sun.
The earth takes a year to make one trip around the sun.

8

During a year the length of our day changes. In winter the days
are short. It may be dark by the time you get home from school.
It is cold because we don't get many hours of sunshine.

As we move into spring, days become a bit longer. By summer they are even longer.

The days may be so long that it is still light when you go to bed. It is warm because we get many hours of sunshine.

After the long days of summer, the days begin to get shorter and cooler. It is fall and time to go back to school.

All through the year the earth has been rotating once in twenty-four hours, giving us day and night. And all through the year the lengths of darkness and daylight have been changing. The seasons have been changing too.

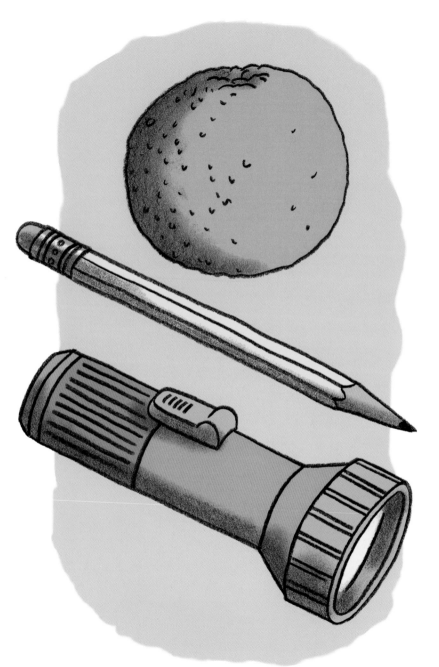

You can see
the reason for
these changes by
using an orange for
the earth, a pencil, and
a flashlight. Push a pencil
through an orange from top
to bottom.

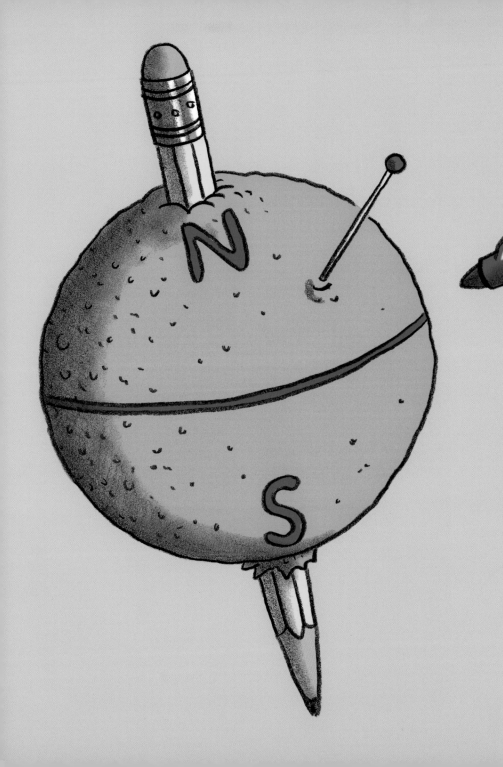

The top is the North Pole. You can mark it with an N. The bottom is the South Pole. Using a marking pen, draw a line around the orange halfway between the poles. That's the equator. Stick a pin in the orange about halfway between the equator and the North Pole. Imagine this is where you live.

Turn the pencil and the orange. The pencil is the axis of the orange.

The earth also has an axis. There is nothing like a pencil through the earth. But the earth spins as though there were something like a pencil running from pole to pole.

Hold the axis of the orange straight up and down. In a
darkened room, have someone shine a flashlight on the orange.

The light is supposed to be the sun. The
part of the orange toward the flashlight is in
daylight. The other half is in darkness.
   Daylight falls on the North Pole and also the
South Pole, even when you spin the orange.

Walk all around the flashlight. Keep the light shining on the orange. That would be the same as the earth going all around the sun. It would be a year. Keep the axis straight up and down.

Wherever you are as you circle the flashlight, the orange is lighted from pole to pole. All through the year and all over the earth, days and nights would be the same length. There would be no change in seasons.

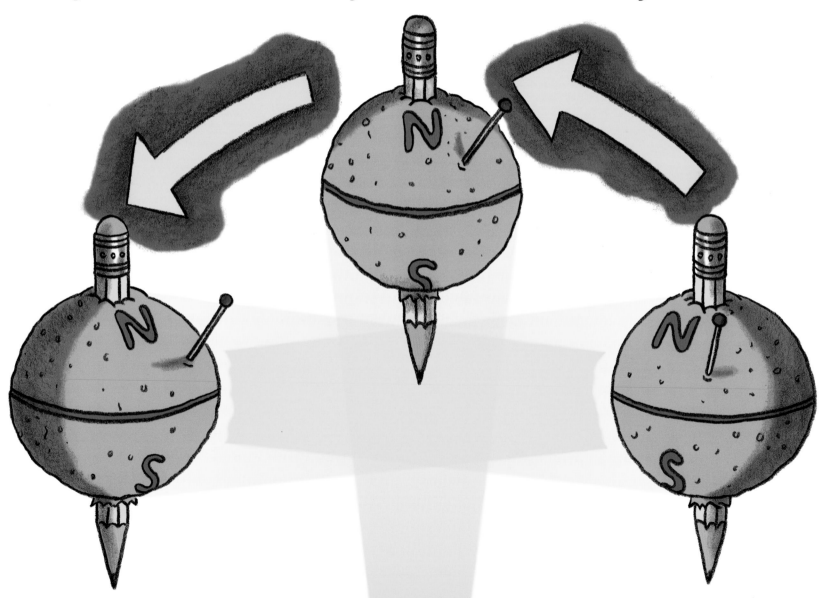

But we know that does not happen on the earth. The days get shorter and then longer as the earth goes around the sun. And winter changes to summer. It's because the axis of the earth is not straight up and down. It is tilted.

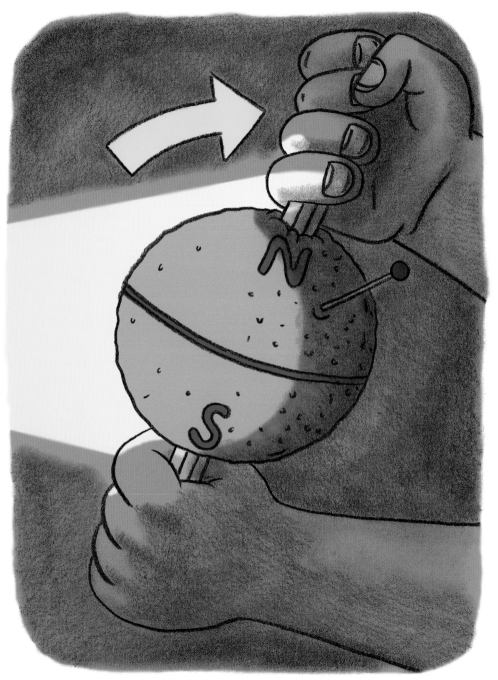

Let's experiment with the orange. This time tilt the axis the way it is tilted in the picture. That's the way the earth's axis is tilted. Hold the orange so the North Pole is tilted away from the flashlight.

Turn the orange all the way around, and you will see that the pin is in the light only a short time. The northern half of the earth has short days and long nights. Sunlight does not fall on the North Pole. The North Pole has its long winter night. It is winter and it is cold.

Keep the axis of the orange tilted in the same direction and go partway around the flashlight. Now the light falls on both poles. It is springtime in the north. Days are getting longer.

22

Without changing the tilt of the axis, move until you are halfway around the flashlight from where you started. Soon the North Pole will be tilted toward the light. It is summer.

As you turn the orange, the pin is in the light longer than it is in the dark. The northern half of the earth has long days and short nights. The North Pole has its long summer day. It is summer and it is warm.

Keep moving around the flashlight. Remember, always keep the orange tilted in the same direction. You'll see that once again light falls on both the North Pole and the South Pole of the orange. It is fall in the north. The days are getting shorter, and cooler too.

Keep moving around and you come back to winter.

They happen because sunshine makes the seasons, and because the axis of the earth is tilted.

The southern half of the earth has seasons too. They are the opposites of our seasons. When it is summer and we are going to the beach, people on the southern half of the earth have winter. They are skating and skiing.

The North Pole and the South Pole also have seasons. Their winters are cold and dark. The sun does not rise every day. It is dark all winter long.

During summer at the poles, the sun does not set every day. For several weeks there is no night.

Seasons at the poles are opposite. When the North Pole has winter, the South Pole has summer. Six months later, when it is winter at the South Pole, it is summer at the North Pole.

Along the equator it is warm all the time. The temperature stays about the same all through the year. You can see why if you experiment with the orange. Move the pin to the equator.

Watch the pin to see what happens as you go through a year. You'll see that day and night are just about the same length in summer and winter, spring and fall.

That's good if you like warm weather all the time. But it's also nice
to see snow once in a while, to see the flowers and birds of springtime,
to go swimming in summer, and have pumpkins in the fall.

Year after year the days change, and so do the seasons. We have winter, spring, summer, and fall because the sun warms the earth. And because the axis of the earth is tilted.

FIND OUT MORE ABOUT THE SUN

- The sun has been giving off light for the last 4.5 billion years.
- Light (traveling at 186,000 miles per second) takes about eight minutes to travel from the sun to the earth.
- The sun's temperature is 10,000 degrees Fahrenheit at the surface and 27,000,000 degrees Fahrenheit at the center.
- The average distance from the earth to the sun is 93,000,000 miles.
- The sun is so large that 1 million planets the size of earth could fit inside it.
- The sun spins around once every 27.4 days.
- The highest temperature ever recorded in the world was 134 degrees Fahrenheit at Death Valley, California, in July 1913.
- The world's highest average temperature—94 degrees Fahrenheit—occurs in Dakol, Ethiopia!
- The lowest temperature recorded on earth was 128.6 degrees below zero Fahrenheit, in Antarctica on July 21, 1983.

FRANKLYN M. BRANLEY was the originator of the Let's-Read-and-Find-Out Science series and the author of close to 150 popular books about scientific topics for young readers of all ages. He was Astronomer Emeritus and former Chairman of the American Museum of Natural History–Hayden Planetarium.

MICHAEL REX is the creator of over thirty books for children, including the #1 *New York Times* bestsellers *Goodnight Goon* and *The Runaway Mummy*, as well as the Fangbone! and Icky Ricky chapter book series. Mr. Rex lives with his family in Bronx, New York. You can visit him online at www.mikerexbooks.blogspot.com.

BE SURE TO LOOK FOR OTHER BOOKS IN THE LET'S-READ-AND-FIND-OUT SCIENCE SERIES:

LEVEL 1

Level 1 books explain simple science concepts for preschoolers and kindergarteners.

CATEGORIES:
The Human Body
Plants
Animals
The World Around Us

LEVEL 2

Level 2 books explore more challenging concepts for children in the primary grades.

CATEGORIES:
The Human Body   Space
Plants   Weather and the Seasons
Animals   Our Earth
Dinosaurs   The World Around Us

Supporting the Common Core Learning Standards and Next Generation Science Standards, Let's-Read-and-Find-Out offers a diverse array of subjects so children may build knowledge, engage in scientific inquiry, and broaden their perspectives. For Common Core resources for this title and others, please visit www.readcommoncore.com.

Find out more at www.letsreadandfindout.com.

US $6.99 / $8.50 CAN
ISBN 978-0-06-238209-2

HARPER
An Imprint of HarperCollinsPublishers
Ages 4 to 8
Cover art © 2005 by Michael Rex

9 780062 382092

50699